JUDY GARLAND & LIZA MINNELLI

A Little Golden Book® Biography

By Phil Stamper • Illustrated by Natalia Sanabria

 A GOLDEN BOOK • NEW YORK
Golden Books
An imprint of Random House Children's Books
A division of Penguin Random House LLC
1745 Broadway, New York, NY 10019
penguinrandomhouse.com
rhcbooks.com

Library of Congress Control Number: 2024952393
ISBN 979-8-217-11644-7 (trade) — ISBN 979-8-217-11645-4 (ebook)
Manufactured in the United States of America
10 9 8 7 6 5 4 3 2 1
EU Contact: Penguin Random House Ireland, 32 Nassau Street, Dublin D02 YH68.
https://eu-contact.penguin.ie

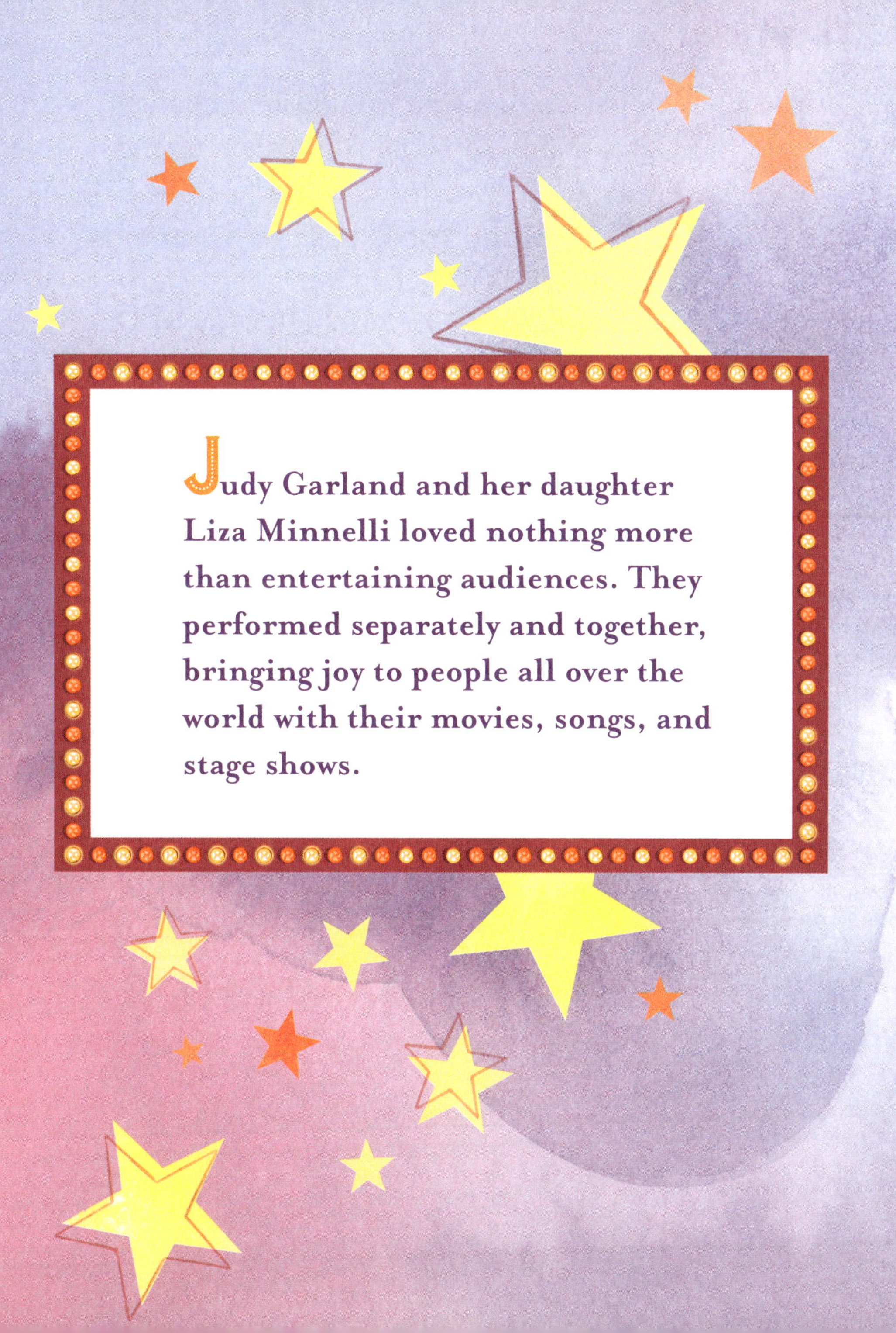

Judy Garland and her daughter Liza Minnelli loved nothing more than entertaining audiences. They performed separately and together, bringing joy to people all over the world with their movies, songs, and stage shows.

Frances Ethel Gumm, who would later be called Judy Garland, was born on June 10, 1922, in Grand Rapids, Minnesota. She was the youngest of three girls. Her parents, Ethel and Frank, traveled the country singing and doing comedy for a living before opening a movie theater in their town.

Sometimes the older sisters performed for audiences at the theater. When Frances was just two years old, she decided to join in the fun. She walked onto the stage during a Christmas show and sang "Jingle Bells."

Frances loved the applause! And she loved making people happy. So she sang the song again . . . and again . . . and again! She was still singing when her father picked her up and carried her away as the crowd laughed and cheered.

Little Frances and her siblings began singing and dancing in local theaters as the Gumm Sisters. All three girls were talented, but everyone knew the youngest was the star!

In 1926, the family moved to California, where there were more opportunities for entertainers. The Gumm Sisters eventually changed their name to the Garland Sisters. Soon after, when Frances was twelve years old, she decided she wanted a new first name, too. She chose Judy.

Judy Garland loved performing onstage with her sisters, but now she had a bigger dream: to be a movie star. After lots of auditions, she signed a contract with the biggest movie studio at the time, Metro-Goldwyn-Mayer (also called MGM).

For the next few years, she appeared in musical comedies and teen films including *Everybody Sing* and *Love Finds Andy Hardy*. Her parts were sometimes small, but she always stole the show with her amazing singing voice.

Then, when Judy was seventeen, she was cast as the lead in a movie unlike anything the world had ever seen.

The Wizard of Oz is a musical fantasy about a Kansas farm girl named Dorothy Gale who finds herself in a magical land. Looking for a way back home, she travels down a yellow brick road with a Scarecrow, a Tin Man, and a Cowardly Lion to ask the Wizard of Oz for help.

Judy was thrilled to play Dorothy. With extravagant sets, costumes, and special effects, *The Wizard of Oz* was a huge production and was one of the first movies filmed in color!

Judy loved the music, especially the hopeful song "Over the Rainbow." Many people relate to Dorothy because of her bravery and her dreams for a better tomorrow. She's so beloved that some special fans refer to themselves as Friends of Dorothy.

The Wizard of Oz premiered in 1939. The movie was a hit, and Judy was a real movie star, just as she had wanted. She was given more leading roles in the years that followed. While filming *Meet Me in St. Louis*, Judy fell in love with the film's director, Vincente Minnelli. In 1945, one year after the movie came out, they got married. Soon, Judy found out she was going to have a baby!

Liza May Minnelli was born on March 12, 1946, in Los Angeles, California. Judy named her after the title of a song from the 1929 musical *Show Girl*.

For the first time in twenty years, Judy took a much-needed break from acting to care for her baby. But it wouldn't be long before Judy—and her daughter—stepped back into the spotlight.

Little Liza loved singing and dancing. When she was three years old, she had her first movie role, alongside her mother. Judy gives Liza a big kiss on the cheek just as the film *In the Good Old Summertime* ends.

As the daughter of a director and a performer, Liza didn't have a typical childhood. She spent a lot of time on movie sets. When she was eleven, she started responding to her mother's fan mail, and by the time she was a teenager, she had attended schools in California, New York, and London.

When she was seventeen, Liza performed with her mom on television. At the time, Judy was the star of a variety program called *The Judy Garland Show.* Judy and Liza sang a beautiful duet. Audiences were impressed.

After many years of doing movies and TV shows, Judy wanted to perform in front of an audience again, like she used to with her sisters.

On two memorable nights in 1964, Liza joined Judy on a famous stage in London, England. They sang popular songs and show tunes including "Hello, Dolly!" and "Over the Rainbow."

Liza was ready to make a name for herself as a performer, so she moved to New York City. She landed her first big Broadway role in *Flora, the Red Menace*, at just nineteen years old. Her proud parents were in the audience on opening night.

She wowed audiences with her singing, dancing, and acting and won a Tony Award for Best Actress in a Musical. Liza was—and still is—the youngest actress to win this award!

Meanwhile, Judy decided to move to London, the city that had always made her feel safe and loved. It was there that Judy Garland died on June 22, 1969. She was only forty-seven years old, but in that time, she made more than thirty movies, recorded many songs and albums, and performed all over the world.

Liza continued entertaining audiences just as her mother would have. In 1972, she starred in a movie musical called *Cabaret*. Liza played a carefree showgirl named Sally Bowles. She won an Oscar for Best Actress for her performance.

Soon after, *Liza with a Z*—one of the first concert films made for television—aired. In it, Liza wore flashy costumes as she danced and sang a variety of musical numbers. The show went on to win four Emmy Awards.

With her signature pixie haircut, long eyelashes, and sparkling outfits, Liza had quickly become a household name.

In 1974, she starred on Broadway in a one-woman show called *Liza*. In 1981, she played the role of Linda Marolla in the hit movie *Arthur*. And from 2003 to 2013, she gained a whole new group of fans thanks to her very funny appearances as Lucille Austero on the TV series *Arrested Development*.

Liza is one of the few performers to get an EGOT. This means she's received each of the four biggest performing arts awards—an Emmy, Grammy, Oscar, and Tony!

There may never be a more talented mother-and-daughter pair than Judy Garland and Liza Minnelli. They will always be remembered for the love they had for each other, their incredible talent, and the joy they brought to people everywhere.